THE WAY OF HUMILITY

JORGE CARDINAL BERGOGLIO

The Way of Humility

Corruption and Sin

On Self-Accusation

Translated by Helena Scott

IGNATIUS PRESS   SAN FRANCISCO

Cover photo by Stefano Spaziani

Cover design by Enrique Javier Aguilar Pinto

Published 2014 by Ignatius Press, San Francisco
All rights reserved
ISBN 978-1-58617-891-8
Library of Congress Control Number 2013917061
Printed in the United States of America ∞

CONTENTS

Corruption and Sin

On Self-Accusation

CORRUPTION AND SIN

Preface

In meetings with archdiocesan and civil organizations in our city, the theme of corruption, as one of life's ongoing factors, keeps coming up. You hear about people and institutions that are visibly corrupt and that have begun to decompose, losing their identity, their capacity to exist, to grow, to approach fulfillment, to serve the whole of society. This is nothing new: ever since the birth of mankind, this phenomenon has always existed. Clearly, it is a process of death: when life dies, there is corruption. I often notice that people talk about corruption and sin as though they were identical, which is not really true. A situation of sin and a state of corruption are two different things, though closely interrelated.

Corruption: "Denounced but Acceptable"

With this in mind, I thought it would be appropriate to republish an article I wrote in 1991. At that time the media were giving a lot of space and time to this topic. It was the time when the Catamarca affair was polarizing the nation's attention, and many people were astonished that such things could happen.[1] Then we started getting used to the word "corruption" and to the fact of it, as if it were just part of daily life. We know that we are all sinners, but the new thing that has now entered the collective imagination is that corruption seems to be part of the normal life of society, an aspect of citizenship that is denounced but acceptable. I don't want to go into details: the newspapers are full of them.

Discerning Corruption

It will do us good to reflect together on the problem of corruption and also on its relationship

---

[1] Investigation of a notorious rape and murder in the Argentinian province of Catamarca in 1991 was hampered by the political authorities, whose family members appeared to be involved; this gave rise to widespread popular protest.

with sin. It will do us good to shake up our souls with the prophetic force of the gospel, which places us in the truth about things by stirring up the layers of the fallen dead leaves of human weakness and complicity that can create the conditions for corruption. It will do us a lot of good, in the light of God's word, to learn to discern the different states of corruption that surround us and threaten to lead us astray. It will do us good to say to one another again, "Yes, I'm a sinner; but no, I'm not corrupt!"— and to say it with fear, lest we accept the state of corruption as just another sin.

The Beauty of Redemptive Humility

"Yes, I'm a sinner." How beautiful it is to be able to feel and to say this and, by doing so, to plunge into the mercy of the Father, who loves us and is waiting for us at every moment. "Yes, I'm a sinner", as the publican said in the Temple ("God, be merciful to me a sinner!" [Lk 18:13]); as Peter felt and said, first in words ("Depart from me, for I am a sinful man, O Lord" [Lk 5:8]) and later in tears, when he heard the cock

crow that night, a moment that the genius of
J. S. Bach captured in the sublime aria "Erbarme
dich, mein Gott" ("Have mercy, my God").
"Yes, I'm a sinner", as the prodigal son of Jesus'
parable said: "I have sinned against heaven and
before you" (Lk 15:21)—and could not go on,
because he was enfolded in his waiting father's
loving embrace. "Yes, I'm a sinner", as the
Church has us say at the beginning of Mass and
every time we look at our crucified Lord. "Yes,
I'm a sinner", as David said when the prophet
Nathan opened his eyes with his truth-telling
(2 Sam 12:13).

Corruption Is Not Open to This Beauty

But how difficult it is for the force of truth to
break open hearts that are corrupt! They are so
wrapped up in their self-sufficiency that they
admit no questioning. A corrupt person is one
who "lays up treasure for himself, and is not
rich toward God" (Lk 12:21). He feels comfort-
able and happy, like the man who was planning
to build new barns (Lk 12:16–21). If the situation becomes difficult, he knows all the excuses

to get himself out of it, like the corrupt steward (Lk 16:1–8), an early practitioner of the philosophy "If you don't steal, it's because you aren't clever enough." Corrupt people are those who have built up their self-esteem on that type of deceitful attitude and go through life taking the shortcuts of self-advantage, at the price of their own true dignity and other people's. Their expression is constantly one of "I didn't do it", with faces as innocent as a holy picture, as my grandmother used to say. They could be awarded honorary doctorates in social cosmetics. And the worst of it is that they end up believing themselves. How difficult it is for any word of truth to find its way into their hearts! Therefore, though we say, "Yes, I'm a sinner", let's shout aloud, "But no, I'm not corrupt!"

The Corrupt Do Not Face Up to the Truth

One of the characteristics of corrupt people when confronted by the truth is that they can never allow themselves to be called into question. At the first sign of criticism they react angrily, deny the right of the person or institution to pass judgment on them, or try to refute any moral authority that dares to question them; they have recourse to sophistries and semantic equivocations, belittle others, and hurl insults at anyone who thinks differently from them (cf. Jn 9:34). Corrupt people generally berate themselves unconsciously and then project the irritation produced by this self-blame onto others, so that they turn from attacking themselves to attacking others.

Evidence in the Gospel

Saint Luke shows the fury of these men (cf. Lk 6:11) on hearing the truth spoken by Jesus: "They were filled with fury and discussed with one another what they might do to Jesus." They persecute others by imposing a rule of terror on all those who oppose them (cf. Jn 9:22) and get their revenge by expelling them from their society (cf. Jn 9:34–35). They are afraid of the light because their souls have become like earthworms, dwelling in darkness, underground. In the Gospel we see corrupt people twisting the truth, laying traps for Jesus (cf.

Jn 8:1–11; Mt 22:15–22; Lk 20:1–8), plotting to get rid of him (cf. Jn 11:45–57), bribing someone to betray him (cf. Mt 26:14–16), or bribing the soldiers on guard (cf. Mt 28:11–15). Saint John describes Jesus in their midst as a light that shines in the darkness, a light that darkness could not overpower or grasp (cf. Jn 1:5). Corrupt individuals cannot grasp the truth. We can reread the Gospels looking for the typical features of these people and their reaction to the light brought by our Lord.

Being Alert to the Dangers of Corruption

In offering this piece to the public once more, I hope that it will prove useful in helping us to understand the danger of the personal and social collapse that corruption brings and will also help us to be vigilant, because a habitual state of everyday complicity with sin can lead us to corruption. The season of Advent is an especially appropriate time for us to be alert for anything that prevents us from opening our hearts to the desire to meet Jesus Christ when he comes. May we allow ourselves to encounter him in order to journey afresh along the path of Christian life.

I would like to thank Father Gustavo O. Carrara in particular for his moral support in producing this publication.

Jorge Mario Cardinal Bergoglio, S.J.
Buenos Aires, December 8, 2005
Solemnity of the Immaculate Conception

Reflections on the Subject
of Corruption

We are reminded that, these days, there is a lot of talk about corruption, especially with regard to politics.[2] The phenomenon is denounced in various sectors of society. Several bishops have pointed to the "moral crisis" currently experienced by many institutions. At the same time, there has been a growing general reaction to certain events whose origins lie in corruption, and in some cases, like the Catamarca affair, given the apparent inability to find a normal solution to the problem, public action has taken the form of demonstrations bordering on a new Fuentcovejuna.[3] It is a time

---

[2] Octavio Frigerio, "Corrupción, un problema político", *La Nación*, March 4, 1991, 7.

[3] For Catamarca, see the footnote in the Preface. In Fuenteovejuna, a village in Spain, in the fifteenth century, a cruel and tyrannical commander was murdered by a united band of the villagers, who were subsequently pardoned by the king. This was the subject of a play of the same name by Lope de Vega.

when the reality of corruption is being brought very noticeably to light.

Getting to the Roots of Corruption

And yet all corruption at the social level is simply the result of a corrupt heart. There would be no social corruption if there were no corrupt hearts: "What comes out of a man is what defiles a man. For from within, out of the heart of man, come evil thoughts, fornication, theft, murder, adultery, coveting, wickedness, deceit, licentiousness, envy, slander, pride, foolishness. All these evil things come from within, and they defile a man" (Mk 7:20–23).

When the Human Heart Does Not Have God as Its Treasure

A corrupt heart: this is where the problem lies. Why does a heart become corrupt? For a human person, the heart is not a dead end, closed on itself; it is not where the give-and-take of relations (including moral relations) stops. On the contrary, the heart is human insofar as it can refer to something else, can adhere, can love or deny love (which is hatred). This is why Jesus, when he invites us to see the heart as the source of our actions, calls our attention to the ultimate direction taken by our questing heart: "Where your treasure is, there will your heart be also" (Mt 6:21). To know a man's heart, to see what state it is in, necessarily involves finding out the treasure with which the heart is concerned, the treasure that liberates and fulfills it or the treasure that destroys and enslaves it—or, in the case at hand, the treasure that corrupts it. From the fact of corruption (whether personal or social), then, we come to the human heart as originator and maintainer of that corruption; and from the heart, we come to the treasure to which that heart is attached.

Method

I would like to reflect on this fact so as to understand it better and also to help prevent the word "corruption" from becoming a mere commonplace, just another word, one of those that are used automatically, emptied of real meaning, by the relativist culture that uses language to reverse true values—the culture that tends to stifle the strength of the one Word. I think that in the first place it may help to get inside the internal structure of the state of corruption by "considering the loathesomeness and the malice ... in itself"[4] in the knowledge that, while corruption is a state that is intrinsically connected to sin, it is distinct from it. In the second place, it is also helpful to discover how a corrupt heart, a corrupt person (as distinct from a sinful person), acts. In the third place, we can go over some of

---

[4] Saint Ignatius, *Spiritual Exercises* (henceforth *SE*), 57 (First Week, Second Exercise, Second Point).

the forms of corruption that Jesus had to face in his time.

Finally, it will help to ask ourselves about the type of corruption that might apply to a religious. Of course, a religious can carry within himself the same kind of corruption as other people, but here I would like to ask about what I would call "minor key" corruption: the possibility, that is, that a religious might have a heart that is corrupt, but (so to speak) only venially, meaning that his loyalties toward Jesus Christ are suffering from a kind of paralysis. Is it possible for a religious to be in some way "partially" or "venially" corrupt?

All these things offer us, methodologically, different viewpoints from which to tackle the theme of corruption. In addition, we should note that "corruption" is a loaded word,[5] charged with contemporary meanings, and there is a risk of forcing our reflection off course to follow these.

---

[5] *"Ein geladenes Wort"*, as von Rad says.

Being Self-Contained

We should not confuse sin and corruption. Sin, especially repeated sin, leads to corruption, but not in a quantitative way (as if so many sins equals one corrupt person), but qualitatively, by creating habits that spoil and limit a person's capacity to love, turning the heart's direction more and more inward toward goals that pertain only to itself, making the person self-contained. As Saint Paul says:

> For what can be known about God is plain to them, because God has shown it to them. Ever since the creation of the world his invisible nature, namely, his eternal power and deity, has been clearly perceived in the things that have been made. So they are without excuse; for although they knew God they did not honor him as God or give thanks to him, but they became futile in their thinking and their senseless minds were darkened. Claiming to be wise, they became fools, and exchanged the glory of the

immortal God for images resembling mortal man
or birds or animals or reptiles. (Rom 1:19–23)

Here we see clearly the process that goes from
sin to corruption, with all that this implies of
blindness, turning away from God to rely on
one's own efforts, and so forth.

It would be fair to say that sins are forgiven
but corruption cannot be forgiven. This is simply because at the bottom of every corrupt
attitude is a weariness with the transcendent:
instead of God, who never tires of forgiving,
the corrupt person sets himself up as sufficient
for his own salvation—he has tired of asking for
forgiveness.

Self-Sufficiency Paralyzes the Heart

Being self-contained is the first characteristic
of all corruption. In the corrupt person there
exists a basic self-sufficiency, which begins
unconsciously and becomes the most natural
thing in the world. Human self-sufficiency is
never an abstract thing. It is an attitude of the
heart that is directed toward a "treasure" that

seduces, tranquilizes, and deceives it, saying, "Soul, you have ample goods laid up for many years; take your ease, eat, drink, be merry" (Lk 12:19). And curiously enough, a contradiction is set up: the self-sufficient person is basically a slave to that treasure, and the more enslaved he is, the more insufficient he feels in that very self-sufficiency.

A Dangerous Imbalance

This explains why corruption cannot stay hidden. The imbalance between the conviction of self-sufficiency and the reality of being enslaved to a treasure cannot be suppressed. It is an imbalance that forces its way out, boils over with its own pressure, and on emerging, gives off the stink produced by its confinement: it smells bad. Yes, corruption stinks of rottenness. When something begins to smell bad, it is because there is a heart stuck between its own self-contained self-sufficiency and the real impossibility of being enough for itself; it is a heart that has gone rotten by clinging too strongly to a treasure that has captured it.

The Ignorance of the Corrupt

Corrupt people do not notice their own corruption. It is the same as when people have bad breath: they seldom realize it themselves. Other people can smell it and need to tell them. Hence, also, it would be hard for someone who is corrupt to escape from that state through inner repentance. Their good spirit in this regard is anesthetized. Generally, our Lord saves them through means of trials that come from situations they experience (illness, loss of money, loss of loved ones, and so forth), and these are what pierce the armor of their corruption and enable grace to enter. Then they can be cured.

Appearances

From this it is apparent that corruption needs to be cured rather than forgiven.[6] It is like one of those embarrassing illnesses that people try to disguise and cover up until the illness can no longer be kept hidden. This at last opens up the possibility of being cured. Corruption should not be confused with vices (although familiarity with vices leads to making them into one's "treasure"). Corrupt people always try to keep up a good appearance: Jesus gives the name of "whitewashed tombs" to one of the most corrupt groups of his time (cf. Mt 23:25–28). Corrupt people cultivate their good manners to the point of fastidiousness so as to cover up their evil habits.[7]

---

[6] "Forgiven", "cured": the words are not accurate and not correct, because all forgiveness heals. I am setting them in opposition to each other here for the sake of helping us to understand the point.

[7] "Among these [partisan] leaders there are some who, like the courtesans of old who acted as vestal virgins, try to escape suspicion [of being corrupt] today by officiating as unexpected guardians of the temple of public morality" (Frigerio, "Corrupción, un problema político").

The Appearance of Being Excusable

The sick attitude of a corrupt person will appear etiolated in his behavior and will look, at worst, like weaknesses or weak points that are relatively admissible and excusable by society. For example, someone who is corrupted with ambition for power will seem, at most, to have a certain tendency to fickleness or superficiality that leads him to change his mind or adapt his behavior depending on the situation; he will be called weak or adaptable or self-interested, but the wound of his corruption (ambition for power) will remain hidden. Another example is someone corrupted by lust or avarice who disguises his condition in forms that are more socially acceptable and appear to be mere pleasure-seeking and frivolity.

The Gravity of Frivolity

But frivolity is in fact a much graver sin than lust or avarice, simply because the frivolous person has permanently set his sights on a short-range objective in a way that is reversible only with great difficulty. Sinners, on recognizing themselves as such, in some way admit the falseness of the treasure to which they were or are attached, whereas the corrupt person has put his vice through a crash course in good manners; he conceals his true treasure not by hiding it from other people's eyes but by refashioning it to be socially acceptable.[8] And his self-sufficiency grows: it begins with fickleness and frivolity and ends up in the conviction, the absolute certainty, that he is better than anyone else:

> He also told this parable to some who trusted in themselves that they were righteous and despised others: "Two men went up into the temple to pray, one a Pharisee and the other a tax collector. The Pharisee stood and prayed thus with himself, 'God, I thank you that I am not like other men, extortioners, unjust, adulterers, or even like this tax collector. I fast twice a week, I give tithes of all that I get.' But the tax collector, standing far off, would not even lift up his eyes to heaven, but beat his breast, saying, 'God,

---

[8] "Beware of practicing your piety before men in order to be seen by them ... sound no trumpet before you, as the hypocrites do in the synagogues and in the streets, that they may be praised ... for they love to stand and pray in the synagogues and at the street corners, that they may be seen.... And when you fast do not look dismal" (Mt 6:1–18).

be merciful to me a sinner!' I tell you, this man went down to his house justified rather than the other; for every one who exalts himself will be humbled, but he who humbles himself will be exalted. (Lk 18:9–14)

Making Comparisons

"Or even like this tax collector": corrupt people constantly need to compare themselves with those who seem to be consistent in their lives (even when it is the consistency of the tax collector in confessing that he is a sinner) so as to cover up their own inconsistency and to justify their own attitude. To a fickle person, for example, someone who tries to hold on to clear, nonnegotiable moral principles is a fundamentalist— old-fashioned, narrow-minded, someone who fails to keep up with the times. And here we see another typical trait of corrupt people: the way they justify themselves.

A Need for Justification

Deep down, corrupt people feel the need to justify themselves, even though they don't actually realize what they are doing. The way that corrupt people justify themselves (i.e., compare themselves with others) has two characteristics. In the first place, it is done with reference to situations that are extreme, exaggerated, or bad in themselves: rapaciousness, injustice, adultery, failure to fast or to pay tithes (as in the above parable). They make reference to something exaggerated or to an undeniable sin and, in that context, set up a comparison between the good manners of their own faults and the severity of the sin to which they refer. The comparison is false, because its terms are of two different kinds: an appearance is compared with a reality. But at the same time they apply to the other person a reality that is not so straightforward.

Caricatures

And here we have their second characteristic: in any comparison, the other person is usually caricatured. Either the person himself is caricatured (as in the case of the Pharisee referring to the tax collector), or else there is a caricature in the connections that are made with external situations, or situations that affect him in some way, through interpretations of facts in the light of other similar facts that are only apparently real or that are real but wrongly applied. (That is the case of the Pharisees' insult to Jesus: "*We* were not born of fornication",[9] or the way they reduced Jesus' actions to those of a mere rebel: "If you release this man, you are not Caesar's friend; every one who makes himself a king sets himself against Caesar."[10] Here, for example, a political note is projected into the comparison.) When we meet justifications of this kind, we can usually assume that we are faced with a case of corruption.

---

[9] Jn 8:39–41 [emphasis added]. Laurentin, discussing this text, cites some exegetes who think that it refers to the Mother of Jesus at the time when she returned to Nazareth from Ain Karim. Her pregnancy was apparent by that time, and this is what led Joseph to want to send her away in secret. Many people would have thought the worst, seeing her as having transgressed the Law. This exegesis is very possible from the biblical viewpoint—and now the Pharisees strike at the Mother of Jesus. I would see no difficulty in accepting that exegesis from the theological point of view, because it would mark still another step in Jesus' self-emptying, and that of his Mother, who accompanied him every step of the way.

[10] Jn 19:12. Obviously there is reductionism in this comparison.

From Comparison to Judgment

On making such comparisons, corrupt people set themselves up in judgment over others: they themselves are the measure of morality.[11] "I am not like this tax collector" means "He is not like me, and I thank you for it."[12] As if to say, "I am the measure of how to fulfill the law: I pay tithes" and so on. But in thus setting themselves up as the measure of all things, there is an underlying danger: no one can twist reality so much without running the risk of that same reality turning against them.

---

[11] To set themselves up as judges, corrupt people try to present themselves as balanced, neither left-wing nor right-wing; and when circumstances compel them to adopt extreme measures that would denote their corruption and show imbalance, they manage to prove that that imbalance was necessary for the sake of a higher order of balance. But never, even in tactical imbalance, do they cease to be the judge of the situation. In this regard, see the comment by Frigerio quoted earlier: "The very corruption of the courtesan turns her into a vestal virgin when it suits her."

[12] In other words, "I thank you that there are so few people like me." Corrupt people try to stand apart from any corporate group; they always feel they are above others.

And from Judgment to Brazen Audacity

And it does turn against them. Being is transcendentally *verum*, true, and I can twist it and wring it like a towel, denying the truth; but being will continue to be true, even if, in the context of a particular situation, someone manages to present it otherwise. Being fights to show itself as it is.[13] At the very heart of the judgment made by a corrupt person, there is set up a lie: a lie about life, a metaphysical lie about being, which in time will turn against the person who made it. On the moral plane, corrupt people avoid this by projecting their evil onto others. But this is merely a temporary solution, which only increases the tension of being to recover its truthfulness (since it never actually lost its truth). And Jesus tells the corrupt man that the evil one is not the other person, but that "your eye is not sound."[14]

---

[13] All creation is striving for this, as if with birth pangs, as Saint Paul says (Rom 8:22).

[14] Mt 6:23. And if it is evil, it would be better to pluck it out.

The Loss of Modesty

Corruption leads to the loss of the modesty that guards the truth and makes it possible for the truth to be truthful. It is modesty that, as well as the truth, guards the goodness, beauty, and unity of being. Corruption works on a different plane from modesty: situating itself on this side of transcendence, it necessarily goes beyond in its pretentiousness and complacency. It has travelled the road all the way from modesty to acceptable shamelessness.[15]

---

[15] Perhaps a comparison may help us to understand this. Stealing a woman's purse is a sin, and the thief is sent to prison, and the woman tells her friends all about it, and everyone agrees that things are in a terrible state and that the public authorities ought to do something about it, because it's not safe to go out. And the woman in question, who had her purse snatched, never even thinks about what her husband is like in business matters, how he cheats the state by not paying taxes, gets rid of his employees every three months to avoid dependency in employment relations, and so on. And her husband, and perhaps she herself, boasts about these business tricks and underhanded dealings. This is what I call acceptable shamelessness. Another instance: prostitution is a sin, and prostitutes are called "women of evil life" or simply "bad women". Socially they are reviled for contaminating culture and corrupting people, et cetera, et cetera. And the same person who says all that goes to a party for the third marriage of a friend (after the friend's second divorce) or accepts that So-and-so has a few "affairs" (provided that they are in good taste) or that this or that film star's love life is published, when the star changes "partners" like a pair of shoes. What I am getting at is that there is a difference between the prostitute and this so-called liberal-minded woman. The prostitute has not lost her shame; the other woman has gone beyond modesty and shame, and her attitude is one of shamelessness, which social convention makes acceptable.

Triumphalism

As well as being judgmental, corruption has
another feature: it grows and at the same time
expresses itself in an atmosphere of triumphalism. Triumphalism is the perfect breeding
ground for corrupt attitudes, because experience
tells people that those sorts of attitudes produce
good results, and so they feel like winners, tri-
umphant. Everything works out well. And feeling good, being on a roll, they rearrange and
reinforce situations with false evaluations.

A False Optimism

That is not triumph but triumphalism. Fickleness and frivolity, for example, are forms of corruption that can germinate comfortably in the
dire atmosphere of what Henri de Lubac calls
"spiritual worldliness",[16] which is quite simply

---

[16] Henri de Lubac, *Méditations sur l'Église* (Paris: Aubier, 1953), 327;
translated by Michael Mason as *The Splendour of the Church* (London:
Sheed and Ward, 1956).

triumph mutated into triumphalism of the human capacity: pagan humanism subtly transformed into Christian common sense. Corrupt people, when integrating into their characters stable situations of the degeneration of being, feel optimistic about their lives because they appear to be going so well, to the extent that they are intoxicated with a triumphalistic eschatology. Corrupt people have no hope. Sinners hope for forgiveness, but corrupt people don't, because they do not feel that they are in sin: they feel that they have triumphed. Christian hope has been reduced to the future possibility of a triumph that has already been achieved, as an inherent possession.[17]

---

[17] This phenomenon of the reduction of hope draws its strength from Joachim de Fiore's teaching about the "Third Age". His concept of the Church was corrupted in that sense. Many systems of "immanent hope" were built up on his teaching. The mystery of the Church was thus reread in the light of particular cultural movements or political events, and in that way a curious fact arose: in the name of progress, of taking a step forward in the development of mankind, transcendence was made into something self-contained, and that self-containment was actually a more dangerous kind of fundamentalism than the sort that involves a misunderstood return to the sources. It was the fundamentalism of immanence, of rereading the mysteries of the Church in terms of political redemption or even in terms of political-cultural aspects of nations, however good these might be in themselves.

The Shifting of Parameters

This triumphalism, born of the feeling that one is the measure of all justice and judgment, gives itself airs and reduces everyone else to the measure of its own triumph. To put it another way: an atmosphere of corruption, a corrupt person, does not allow anyone to grow freely. Corrupt people know nothing of fraternity or friendship, only complicity. Loving one's enemies, or even the distinction between friends and enemies that was at the basis of the Old Law, are meaningless to corrupt people. Their parameters are different: for them, you are either an accomplice or an enemy. For example, when a corrupt person is in power, he will always implicate others in his own corruption, bring them down to his measure, and make them accomplices of his chosen way of doing things.[18]

Corruption Has Its Own Proselytism

And all this is done in an atmosphere that is imposed on all: a triumphalist atmosphere, an

---

[18] It is no longer just a measure with regard to value judgment, but also a measure of association or of reference to the coming together of followers. To be fellow soldiers with him, they have to be his accomplices.

atmosphere of "bread and circuses", with an appearance of common sense in judging things and of the practical feasibility of the chosen options. Since corruption includes the assumption of being oneself the measure of things, all corruption proselytizes, pulls others in. Sin and temptation are contagious, but corruption actively proselytizes.[19]

Ensnaring Others in the State of Corruption

This proselytizing dimension of corruption points to its active nature and its skill in gathering others. It fits perfectly into the campaign plan of Lucifer, its leader, as presented by Saint Ignatius in the *Spiritual Exercises*. The aim of gathering others is not to make them commit sins, but rather to ensnare men in the state of sin, in the state of corruption: "in chains ... first to tempt men with the lust of riches ... that they

---

[19] There are three characteristics of all temptation to sin: the temptation *grows*, it is *contagious*, and it is *self-justifying*. These same characteristics also appear, but in a different way, in the state of corruption. Corruption is *consolidated, gathers others*, and *establishes laws*. The *growth* of temptation now becomes a process of consolidation; the *contagiousness* of temptation becomes active proselytizing; and finally, the simple *self-justification* of temptation is developed and worked up into established laws.

may thereby more easily gain the empty honor of the world [i.e., triumphalism] and then come to unbounded pride." [20] It is a plan to create a condition strong enough to resist the invitation to grace, both now (the First Class) and always (the Second Class).[21]

---

[20] *SE*, 76 (Second Week, Fourth Day, Meditation on Two Standards).

[21] *SE*, 78 (Second Week, Fourth Day, Meditation on the Three Classes of Men). Here the reference is forced, because in this case it does not appear that the men acquired the riches through corruption, but simply that they acquired them "not purely, as they should have, for love of God" (*SE*, 77, Fourth Day, Meditation on the Three Classes of Men, First Prelude). But it does serve as an example.

In Jesus' Time

In the New Testament we find corrupt people whose adherence to the state of sin is clear at a glance. Such is the case of Herod the Great (Mt 2:3–15) and Herodias (Mt 14:3ff.; Mk 6:19). In others, corruption is disguised as socially acceptable attitudes: for instance, the case of Herod Antipas, who listened to John the Baptist and "heard him gladly" (Mk 6:20), but opted for perplexity as a façade to defend his corruption; or Pilate, who acted as though the matter had nothing to do with him and so washed his hands (Mt 27:24), but underneath it all, did so in order to defend his corrupt aim of clinging to power at all costs.

Corruption among the Jews of Jesus' Time

But in Jesus' time there are also corrupt groups: the Pharisees, the Sadducees, the Essenes, the

Zealots.[22] A look at these groups will help us to comprehend the fact of the corruption that opposed Jesus Christ himself and his message of salvation. These four groups have two features in common. In the first place they have all drawn up a system of teaching to justify or to cover up their corruption. The second feature: these groups go as far as they can to oppose sinners and the people, without actually declaring themselves their enemies. Not only do they consider themselves clean, but by that very attitude they proclaim their cleanliness.

Complex Corruption Causes Division

The Pharisees devise a system of teaching about how to fulfill the law with an exaggerated degree of particular detail, and that leads them to despise sinners, whom they consider breakers of this crushing law (Mt 23:13ff.). The Sadducees see sinners and the common

---

[22] In this regard see Kurt Schubert, *Die jüdischen Religionsparteien in neutestamentlicher Zeit*. Here I simply give a very general and even simplified description of the matter, merely seeking to exemplify the case of the corruption of elites.

people as small-fry, unable to negotiate with power at the various junctures of life; and into their doctrine of negotiation with the ruling power they put their own inner corruption, leaving no room for the hope that transcends this life. The Zealots seek a political solution, here and now. That is their teaching, and it conceals a large dose of social resentment and the absence of a theological understanding of their times. For them, their people's theology of exile is no longer valid; and "the sinners", the common people, will end up as "useful idiots" whom they will summon to be indoctrinated into an armed struggle. Finally, at first glance it is difficult to see corruption in the Essenes, because they are men of very good will who seek in monastic life recollection and salvation for a chosen group. Their corruption lies in this: they have been tempted under the appearance of good and have allowed that temptation to be consolidated as the doctrinal reference point for their lives. For them, sinners and the common people are outside that plan and are unsuitable to swell the numbers of their group.

Jesus' Response

The answer given by Jesus to John the Baptist is, over and above the Baptist himself, directed at them: "Go and tell John what you have seen and heard: the blind receive their sight, the lame walk, lepers are cleansed, and the deaf hear, the dead are raised up, the poor have good news preached to them" (Lk 7:22).

Jesus stands, then, against these four groups, these four currents of corrupt doctrine, and recalls the promises of redemption made to his people (cf. Is 26:19; 42:7; 61:1). He has recourse to the patrimony of his people, the Scriptures, as he did when he was tempted in the desert. He rereads the Scriptures because it is they that bear witness to him (Jn 5:39), as against the alternatives proposed by those four elites.

Summing Up

Corruption is not an act but a state, a personal and collective state, to which people get accustomed and in which they live. The values (or non-values) of corruption are integrated into a real culture, with a capacity for its own systematic doctrine, its own language, and its own particular way of acting. It is a culture of pygmyism, inasmuch as it gathers proselytes to bring them down to the level of admitted complicity.

A False and Destructive Culture

This culture has a dual dynamism: appearance and reality, immanence and transcendence. The appearance is not the breaking out of reality by way of truthfulness; it is the constructing of a reality in such a way that it can be imposed and accepted as widely as possible in society. It is a culture of taking away; reality is taken away

45

and replaced by appearance. Transcendence becomes steadily more "here and now", practically immanent; or, at most, an armchair transcendence. Being is no longer protected but is ill-treated through a kind of socially acceptable shamelessness. In the culture of corruption there is a lot of shamelessness, even though what is allowable in the corrupt atmosphere is fixed in severe, almost Victorian rules of conduct. As I said, it is a culture of good manners covering up evil habits. And that culture is imposed in the laissez-faire of everyday triumphalism.

Openness to Forgiveness

People do not always become corrupt in one go. In fact, it is generally just the opposite. It is a slippery slope. And that slope is not always a clearly sinful path. It is possible for someone to be a great sinner and yet never fall into corruption. That may have been the case of Zacchaeus, Matthew, the Samaritan woman, Nicodemus, and the Good Thief, who had something in their sinful hearts that saved them from corruption. The clinging to self-containment that

is characteristic of corrupt people had not yet
taken shape in them; they were still open to
forgiveness. Their deeds were born of a sinful
heart; many of them were evil deeds, but at the
same time the heart that produced them could
feel its own weakness. And that was where
God's strength could find a way in. "The foolishness of God is wiser than men, and the weakness of God is stronger than men" (1 Cor 1:25).

I have been making a distinction, which may
be dangerous, between sin and corruption; still,
all in all, it is a true one. And yet it has to be
said that the path that leads to corruption is sin.
How so? It is a subtle kind of progression, or
rather a qualitative leap from sin to corruption.
The author of the letter to the Hebrews tells us:
"See to it that no one fail to obtain the grace
of God; that no 'root of bitterness' spring up
and cause trouble, and by it the many become
defiled" (Heb 12:15). Obviously he is speaking
here of something more than sin; he is pointing
out a state of corruption. Ananias and Sapphira
sinned, but it was not the sin of weakness of
heart, but of corruption: they were cheating,
trying to trick God (Acts 5:4), and they were

punished precisely because of the corruption created in them by their fraudulent action.

The Wisdom of Saint Ignatius

Should we then start trying to tell the difference between sin and corruption? I don't think it would help much. What has been said up to now is quite enough. It is possible for someone to sin repeatedly and yet not be corrupt; but, at the same time, the repetition of sin can lead to corruption. Saint Ignatius understands this and hence does not stop at knowledge of our own sins but takes us further, to knowledge and hatred of our disordered actions and of all things that are worldly and vain.[23] He knows the danger of the "root of bitterness" that "causes trouble". For those making the *Spiritual Exercises*, he seeks states of soul that are open to transcendence in their attachment to our Lord and that do not hold on to any area of self-containment.

---

[23] *SE*, 58 (First Week, Third Exercise, First Colloquy).

The Corruption of Religious

Corruptio optimi pessima—the worst corruption is the corruption of the best. This can be applied to religious who are corrupt. They do exist. They existed in the past, as we can see from reading history. In the various religious orders that asked for reform or undertook it, the problem of corruption had been present to a greater or lesser extent. I don't want to talk here about obvious cases of corruption, but rather about everyday states of corruption, which I would call venial, but which bring the flow of religious life to a halt. How do these come about?

The Closing of the Soul

Blessed Peter Faber gave a golden rule for detecting the state of a soul that was living tranquilly and at peace: to propose to that person

something *more* (*magis*).[24] The person whose
soul was closed to generosity would react
badly. The soul gets used to the bad smell of
corruption. The same thing happens in a closed
space: only someone who comes in from outside notices the bad smell in the air. And when
someone tries to help a person in that state, the
amount of resistance is indescribable.

The Israelites were slaves in Egypt, but they
had gotten used to their loss of freedom, had
adapted the shape of their souls to it, and had
no ambition for any other way of living. Their
consciences were asleep, and in that sense, we
could say there was a certain degree of corruption. When Moses announced God's plan to the
Israelites, "they did not listen to Moses, because
of their broken spirit and their cruel bondage"
(Ex 6:9). When difficulties came up over their
escape from Egypt, they reproached Moses for
having placed himself and them in that situation: "They met Moses and Aaron, who were
waiting for them, as they came forth from Pharaoh; and they said to them, 'The Lord look

---

[24] Blessed Peter Faber, *Memorial*, no. 151.

upon you and judge, because you have made us offensive in the sight of Pharaoh and his servants, and have put a sword in their hand to kill us' " (Ex 5:20–21).

Judith, Jonah, and Elijah

Much later, the elders of Israel, tired and fearful during a siege, wished to make a pact with the enemy, and Judith had to come and reread their history to them to stop them from accepting, like lambs condemned to slaughter, situations that were contrary to God's will (Jud 8:9ff). Jonah wanted to avoid trouble: he was ordered to go to Nineveh, and he set off for Tarshish (Jon 1:2–3), and God had to intervene with a long, purifying ordeal (a real night in the belly of the fish, a type of the night that lasted from the ninth hour of Good Friday to the dawn of the first day of the week). Elijah told himself that he had gone too far in the matter of slaughtering the priests of Baal, and he was overcome with fear of a woman (it reminds *me of* the Twelfth Rule for the Discernment of Spirits for the First Week of the *Spiritual Exercises*) and took to flight and wished to die (1 Kings 19:4); he was unable to bear the loneliness of a triumph in God.

The Result of Long Suffering

Nathanael found it easier to say skeptically that nothing good could come from Nazareth (Jn 1:46) than to believe Philip's enthusiasm. The two disciples, like other Jonahs, also wanted to avoid trouble: they had been told to go to Galilee, and they ran away to Emmaus (Lk 24:13). The rest of the apostles preferred not to believe the evidence of their eyes in the Upper Room, and the evangelist says that "they still disbelieved for joy" (Lk 24:41). That is the heart of the matter: the process of suffering always brings people down; the experience of defeat leads the human heart to become accustomed to it so as not to be surprised or to suffer again if another defeat occurs. Or people simply content themselves with the state they are in and do not want any more trouble.

In all these biblical references we find reluctance. The heart doesn't want any complications.

People are afraid that God will get in and start them along paths that are beyond their control. They are afraid of God's visitation, afraid of his consolation. This engenders a sort of fatalism: their horizons become narrower to fit their loneliness or passivity. They are afraid of ambition and prefer the realism of less to the promise of something more, and they forget that God's most real realism is expressed in a promise: "Go from your country and your kindred and your father's house to the land that I will show you. And I will make of you a great nation, and I will bless you, and make your name great, so that you will be a blessing" (Gen 12:1–2).

A Subtle Corruption

In the apparent realism of preferring less, a subtle process of corruption is already at work: people sink into mediocrity and lukewarmness (two forms of spiritual corruption) and into bargaining with God along the lines of the First and Second Classes of Men referred to earlier. In penitential prayer, in the sacrament of reconciliation, they ask God for forgiveness for other

sins, but they do not lay bare this disillusioned
state of their soul before the Lord. This is the
slow but fatal sclerosis of the heart. Then the
soul begins to satisfy its hunger with the prod-
ucts on offer in the supermarket of religious
consumerism. More than ever, such people live
the consecrated life as a self-contained fulfillment of their personalities.

Corruption Closes the Soul to Transcendence

Many of them will find this self-fulfillment in
job satisfaction, others in their success in works,
others in the pleasure they get out of being
highly regarded; others will seek by perfecting
modern means to fill up the emptiness that their
souls experience with respect to the final end
that they once sought and allowed themselves
to be sought by. Others will do it by leading
an intense social life; they love going out, taking holidays with friends, attending lunches
and receptions; they will try to be taken into
account in everything that means cutting a fig-
ure in the world. I could go on listing cases of
corruption; but, to simplify, all of that is only

part of something deeper: the "spiritual world-liness" referred to earlier.[25]

Spiritual worldliness is paganism in an ecclesi-astical disguise. In contrast with men and women who are corrupt in their consecrated life, the Church shows the greatness of her saints, who have learned how to transcend all appearances, until they contemplate the face of Jesus Christ, and that has driven them "mad for Christ".[26]

---

[25] Spiritual worldliness is "the greatest danger, the most treacherous temptation, which is always reborn insidiously when all the others have been overcome and draws new strength from those very victories" (de Lubac, *Méditations sur l'Église*). De Lubac also defines it as "that which presents itself practically as a detachment from the other kind of worldliness, but whose moral and even spiritual ideal would be, instead of the glory of the Lord, man and his self-perfecting. Spiritual worldliness is nothing other than a radically anthropocentric attitude. This attitude would be irremediable in the case—supposing it possible—of a man endowed with all spiritual perfections who did not refer them to God. If that spiritual worldliness invaded the Church and worked to corrupt her by attacking her in her very principle, it would be infinitely more disastrous than any other merely moral worldliness. Worse still than the foul leprosy that, at certain moments in history, so cruelly disfigured the beloved Spouse, when religion appeared to set up scandal in the sanctuary itself, and, represented by a libertine Pope, hid the face of Jesus Christ under precious stones, cosmetics and spies.... A subtle humanism that is the enemy of the Living God—and, secretly, no less the enemy of man—can install itself in us by a thousand subterfuges" (ibid.).

[26] Peter-Hans Kolvenbach S.J., "Locos por Cristo", *CIS* (*Review of Ignatian Spirituality*) 20, nos. 1–2 (63–64) (1990): 72–89. Also published in Kolvenbach, *Decir al Indecible: estudios sobre los Ejercicios Espirituales de San Ignacio* (Bilbao: Mensajero/Sal Terrae, 1999), 115–32.

Many men and women go through life in venial corruption, which clashes with their consecration; their souls lie by the pool, watching—for thirty-eight years—how the waters are stirred and others are cured (Jn 5:5). Such hearts are corrupt. Someone there is daydreaming and wishing he could bring the dead part of his heart back to life; he hears the Lord's invitation ... but no, it's too much trouble, too much like hard work. Our inner poverty needs to make a bit of an effort to open a space to transcendence, but the sickness of corruption holds us back: *Ad laborem indigentia cogebat, et laborem infirmitas recusabat*: her poverty compelled her to work, and her sickness prevented her from working.[27] And our Lord does not tire of calling, "Do not be afraid." Don't be afraid of what? Don't be afraid of hope ... and hope does not disappoint us (cf. Rom 5:5).

---

[27] Saint Augustine, addressing the Samaritan woman in *Tractates on the Gospel of John*, 15, 17, *CCL*, 36:156.

ON SELF-ACCUSATION

Preface

In commencing the Archdiocesan Assembly, I asked that we would place ourselves in a spirit of prayer, that we would pray very much for the assembly and that we would offer, with a penitential attitude, some sacrifice to our Lord, some mortification to accompany our prayer during this time. I suggested that this sacrifice might be that of not speaking badly of one another. I am aware that we find this difficult, thus I think it is a good thing to offer up. The spirit of the unity of the Church is harmed by backbiting and criticism. Saint Augustine described it as follows: "There are men who judge rashly, who slander, whisper, and murmur, who are eager to suspect what they do not see and eager to spread abroad things they do not even suspect" (*Sermon* 47:12). Negative criticism leads us to focus on the faults and failings of other people; as a result, we can feel superior. The prayer of the Pharisee in the

Temple with the publican (Lk 18:11–12) illustrates this, and Jesus warned us against looking for the speck in someone else's eye and ignoring the plank in our own (cf. Mt 7:3).

Speaking badly of others is harmful for the whole Church because it doesn't stop there: it moves on to become aggression (at least in our hearts). Saint Augustine calls backbiters "men without remedy": "Men without remedy are those who cease to concentrate on their own sins in order to focus on other people's. They look not for something to correct, but for something they can criticize. And, being themselves without excuse, they are always ready to accuse other people" (*Sermon* 19). And, he says, "the only thing that remains to them is the sickness of animosity, and the more they think this makes them strong, the weaker they are rendered by their sickness" (*Commentary on Psalm 32*, 29). To guard against this bad spirit (of speaking badly of others), Christian tradition, from the first Desert Fathers onward, proposes the practice of self-accusation.

Many years ago I wrote an article on the subject of self-accusation. Although it was addressed to young religious, I think it may be good for all of us. I offer it as a contribution to this assembly. The article was inspired by some of the writings of Saint Dorotheus of Gaza, which are added at the end to complete it.

May our Lord help us to progress in the Archdiocesan Assembly in a spirit of prayer, offering the sacrifice of not speaking badly of one another.

Jorge Mario Cardinal Bergoglio, S.J.
Buenos Aires, July 16, 2005
Feast of Our Lady of Mount Carmel

Self-Accusation

The reflections of Saint Dorotheus of Gaza provide us with an opportunity to raise the subject of self-accusation and its effect on the spiritual life, and especially the effect it has on the union of hearts within a community.

It is not rare to find in communities, whether at the local or the provincial level, groups that aim to impose their own thinking and preferences on everyone else. This tends to happen when loving openness to our neighbor is replaced by attachment to our own ideas. Then we defend not the family as a whole but just "my part" of it. We give our allegiance not to the unity that shapes and builds up the body of Christ, but to conflict that divides, separates, and weakens. And for formators and superiors, it is not always easy to form in people a sense of belonging to a family,

First published in the *Boletín de Espiritualidad*, no. 87 (May–June 1984), by the Argentinian Province of the Society of Jesus.

a family spirit, especially when it is a question of forming inner attitudes that are small in themselves but have repercussions at the level of the institution, of the body as a whole.

One of the solid attitudes that needs to be formed in the heart of young religious is that of *self-accusation*, because an absence of self-accusation is what causes partisanship and divisions.

Throughout this essay I will be quoting various passages from the works of Saint Dorotheus of Gaza, preceded by a short consideration of the effects of an attitude of self-accusation.

Self-Accusation Is an Act of Courage

In the first place we need to discard any element of the hypocritical idea that self-accusation is childish, cowardly, or somehow neurotic. On the contrary, self-accusation requires uncommon courage in order to open the door to the discovery of things we do not know about ourselves and let other people see beyond our façade. It means doing away with cosmetics, so that the truth can be plainly shown.

At the basis of self-accusation (which is a means to an end) lies a fundamental choice against individualism, a choice instead of the family spirit of the Church, which leads us to behave as good sons and daughters, good brothers and sisters, so as to become, in due course, good spiritual fathers and mothers. Self-accusation implies a fundamentally communal outlook.

The Dangers of Individualism

When individualism grows, it leads to partisanship within community life. The temptation to individualism starts with a truth (which may be real, or partly real, or only apparent, or completely false).[1] It is generally a "reason"

---

[1] The devil does not use only lies to tempt us. A temptation may well be based on something true but taken in a bad spirit. As Blessed Peter Faber explained: "I felt another desire in the Mass, to wit, that all the good that I might do, or think, or set in hand, etc., should be done in a good spirit, and not through means of a bad one. From there I went on to think how our Lord would not consider it good to reform some things in the Church after the manner of heretics; because, although they (like the devils) say many things that are true, they do not say them with the Spirit of Truth, which is the Holy Spirit" (*Memorial*, no. 51; cf. notes 84 and 375 of the Spanish edition, published by Ediciones Diego de Torres, San Miguel, 1983). Ideologies are largely built up on that basis. Although an ideology is apparently born of a truth, or at least of an opinion, in reality it is born of the will (or as Peter Faber puts it, of a bad spirit). Hence an ideology should always be judged not on its content but on the underlying spirit, which is, precisely, not the spirit of truth.

that both justifies and soothes us. And that "reason" is rooted in the spirit of suspiciousness and
supposition.

Suppositions are like daydreams; they are
always a temptation. God is not in them, because
he is the Lord of real time, the measurable past
and the actual present. As for the future, he is
the Lord of the Promise, who asks us for trust
and abandonment.

The spirit of suspicion and supposition aims
basically for a truth that asserts me against my
brother. It is always a truth that defends me
against community participation, that justifies
my not taking part in the community.

In the teaching of Dorotheus of Gaza it is
the devil himself who sows suspicion in people's hearts in order to divide them from one
another. This phenomenon is the inverse of
that resulting from the Incarnation of the
Word: the devil aims to *divide* (through means
of suspicion) in order to *confuse*; our Lord, by
contrast, is always God and man, *indivise et
inconfuse*—without division of person, without confusion of natures. When the devil sows
suspicion, he tries to convince us by means

fallacies,[2] or half-truths, to manipulate our hearts into selfish convictions that lead us into a world closed off from all objectivity.[3]

Suspicion, sown by the devil, sets up in the heart a crooked measuring rod, which displaces reality. It is not easy to straighten out a religious who is tempted by the possession of a crooked measure of this kind. It is no longer a question of sorting out this or that wrong idea, but a whole hermeneutic—the way he interprets everything. Everything that happens he interprets in a twisted way, because the measure he applies to it is itself crooked.

In this [publication], I have sometimes referred to the statement "They had no right to do this to me", used by discontented nuns, which Saint Teresa of Avila said[4] does so much harm in religious life. Religious who are tempted in this way end up being "collectors of injustices". They spend their lives keeping a careful list of all the injuries that others have

---

[2] Cf. *SE*, 129 ("Rules for Discernment of Spirits", First Week, Second Rule) and 133 (Second Week, Fourth Rule).

[3] Cf. *SE*, 132 ("Rules for the Discernment of Spirits", First Week, Thirteenth Rule).

[4] Cf. *The Way of Perfection*, chap. 13.

done them or that they think others have done them. This frequently leads to a conspiracy-victim spirituality.

In sociology, the conspiracy theory, from a hermeneutical point of view, is the weakest type of hermeneutic there is. It cannot stand up to serious reasoning. It is a primary form of seduction, affecting persons who basically long for a simple division between good and bad (and count themselves among the good). Becoming disconnected from objective reality, they wall themselves up in a sort of defensive ideology. They swap doctrine for this ideology and exchange the patient pilgrimage of God's children for the complex of being victims of a conspiracy set up against them by others—the wicked, the powerful, their superiors, the other members of their community. They end up trapped in a prison of words, and this accords with what Cardinal Tomáš Špidlík said: words born of the mind are a wall, while words born of the heart are a bridge.

We can say that these men's minds are sick. And when we confuse the mind with intellectual capacity, we forget that the mind is damaged by original sin. As Jean Daniélou said, how many people there are who take pride in their intellectual capacity and forget that their minds are deeply wounded, sick, and destructive (because a damaged mind also damages the minds of those around it). But let us not forget that a mind becomes sick and continues to be sick because of a passion that "imprisons the truth" (cf. Rom 1:18ff.).

Anxiety: The Loss of Peace

Alongside that attitude there grows a state of anxiety that is also a bad spirit. Those who have fallen into the habit of being suspicious about everything little by little lose the peace of mind that comes from trusting confidence in God. The right way toward conflict resolution, they imagine, must always pass through the filter of their constant control. They are continually shaken by anxiety, the result of their combination of anger and laziness.

They follow Herod, who was "troubled" (cf. Mt 2:3), and the high priests and the Pharisees who in their agitation tried to put a limit on the power of God by sealing up the tomb (cf. Mt 27:62–66). They want to find a solution to all their fears in the illusion of their own omnipotent control, and they know nothing of God's sweetness, which renders the power of his enemies merely relative, reducing them to smoldering stumps: "[The king's] heart and the heart of his people shook as the trees of the forest shake before the wind. And the Lord said … 'Take heed, be quiet, do not fear, and do not let your heart be faint because of these two smoldering stumps of firebrands'" (Is 7:2–4).

A Hidden Self-Indulgence

This mechanism of suspicion and supposition, cloaked in love for the truth, hides a particular kind of self-indulgence. Behind all their ideas such religious are trying to conceal their self-will. They are habitually overcritical, and with their storm of arguments, all they really prove is their adherence to hidden self-gratification.

Suspicion and supposition lead men to the classic bitterness of those who are ready to accuse God—Dorotheus of Gaza highlights

this in the case of Adam and Eve. Little by little such religious turn away from the truth and
become entangled in lies. There is also, at the
bottom of this enlisting on the side of lies, a dis-
placement of the capacity for condemnation, in
ability to condemn rightly. They confuse bat-
tle with noise and clamor. They have not, as
Saint Ignatius teaches, prayed for the grace to
"have a thorough knowledge of [their] sins and
a feeling of abhorrence for them".[5] Curiously,
they are usually ethicists who counterbalance
the guilt produced in them by their suspicion
of everyone with an affected pretense of not
condemning anyone or anything. Because they
lack all sense of objectivity, their imaginations
condemn a priori as suspect all attempts by
others to come close to them in their personal
lives.

Self-Accusation: A Preemption and a Remedy

The spiritual teaching of self-accusation or
self-contempt, expounded by Saint Dorotheus

---

[5] *SE*, 58 (First Week, Third Exercise, Triple Colloquy).

of Gaza, aims to nip all such temptations in the bud and, echoing the tradition he received from the Fathers of the Church, to place the religious within the objective truth of his relations to God and to other people. The constant exercise of self-accusation forestalls all suspicion and leaves room for the action of God, the one who ultimately brings about the union of hearts.

By self-accusation the heart of the religious abases itself, and it is precisely that inner self-abasement that enables all other natural and technical means of mutual understanding to be effective.

This attitude of abasement has a theological foundation in the self-abasement (*synkatábasis*, literally "condescension") of the Word, which is what makes our access to God possible.[6] Therefore it is Christ himself who gives us access to our brother, beginning with our own self-abasement.

This is the truly Christian way of getting close to someone. This way of getting close to

---

[6]See the theology of the Letter to the Hebrews: 2:17; 3:7ff.; 4:14–16; 9.

someone has a qualitative element that lifts all religious closeness (filial, fraternal, and paternal) into the eschatological sphere, where it is a reality both now and forever.

Additionally, it is our Lord himself who justifies this self-abasement on our part. The Pharisees justified themselves ("you ... receive glory from one another" [Jn 5:44]).The just man seeks justification only from God, and therefore he abases and accuses himself. And just as justification was given to us through Christ's Cross, in a universal and unrepeatable way, our walking along the path of our Lord means that we too must take up the self-abasement of the cross. Self-accusation means accepting the role of the guilty person, as our Lord accepted it and was burdened with our guilt. Man feels guilty, deserving of punishment. Hence Saint Ignatius takes care to recommend that "a person who is in consolation should take care to humiliate and abase himself"[7] lest the pursuit of consolations should lead him to believe he has merits he does not really possess.

---

[7] Cf. SE, 131 ("Rules for the Discernment of Spirits", First Week, Eleventh Rule).

Humiliation and Humility

Self-accusation is always an act of humiliation that leads to humility. And when one opts for the path of humiliation, he is necessarily opting for fighting and victory. As Maximus the Confessor said, the *synkatábasis* of the Word is a lure for the devil, who swallows the bait and dies. "Thus he offers his flesh as a bait to the insatiable hunger of hell's dragon, arousing its greed; and the bait, once swallowed, becomes mortal poison and, because of the power of the divinity within it, causes the dragon's total downfall; that same power would serve, by contrast, as a remedy for human nature, restoring it to its original dignity" (*Centuries* 1.12). Humiliating oneself means somehow attracting the devil's attention, fighting, subjecting oneself to temptation, but in the end, winning.

This attitude, unlike the suspiciousness that produces anxiety, leads to meekness and patience. The rules of modesty written by Saint Ignatius are based on a paragraph in the *Constitutions* that describe this state of meekness:

Let all take special care to guard the doors of their senses very diligently, especially their eyes and ears and tongue, from all disorder; and to keep their soul in peace and true humility, shown in silence when silence should be kept, and, when it is necessary to speak, in considerate and edifying speech, and in the modesty of their faces and the maturity of their gait and all their movements, free from all sign of impatience or pride; trying and desiring to give place to others, valuing all others from the heart as superior to themselves, and outwardly showing them the respect and reverence due to each person's position, with mildness and religious simplicity; so that by consideration for one another they may grow in devotion, and praise God our Lord, whom each should try to recognize in the other, as in his image. (*Constitutions* 250)

This text recalls chapter 12 of the Letter to the Romans and many other Pauline passages that speak of the "fruits of the Spirit". And it is precisely along this path of self-accusation that we reach the further conviction that Saint Ignatius had of himself: he was "nothing but an obstacle".

Christian meekness is built up like that; it goes beyond the sphere of the rules of good manners to attain its deepest root and its perfect model in the meekness of the Lamb.

Someone who accuses himself makes room for God's mercy to enter. He is like the publican who does not dare to raise his eyes (cf. Lk 18:13). Someone who accuses himself is a man who will always come close to others, like the Good Samaritan, and in that way of coming close, Christ himself provides access to others.

It may help us to understand all these things if we read slowly chapters 2 and 3 of book 2 of *The Imitation of Christ*, about humble submission and the good and peaceful man.

Dorotheus of Gaza on Self-Accusation

The numbers given below are those used in the Sources Chrétiennes edition: Dorothée de Gaza, *Oeuvres Spirituelles* (Paris: Du Cerf, 1963).

Instruction 7

79. We should consider, brethren, why it sometimes happens that something unpleasant is said to us, and we remain quite untroubled, as though we had not heard it; and at other times, we instantly get upset. What is the reason for the difference? There are, I believe, many reasons, but I think that one alone is at the root of all the others. Let me explain. For example, one brother has just finished his prayer or has made a good meditation, and so is "in good form". And he puts up with what his brother has said to him and carries on with his affairs without minding it. Another is attached to his brother, and because of that liking, he peacefully accepts whatever

comes to him from that brother. And it also happens that a brother despises the one who says the unpleasant thing and considers whatever comes from that person as beneath contempt, not even rating him as a person and taking no account of him or anything that he may say or do.

80. In the monastery, before I left it, there was a brother whom I never saw upset or annoyed at anyone. What is more, I saw that many of the brothers mistreated him and insulted him in different ways. This young monk bore with whatever anybody did to him as though nobody troubled him at all. I never ceased to admire his remarkable patience and wondered how he had acquired such virtue. One day I called him apart and, making a deep bow, asked him to tell me what thoughts he had in his heart when he showed such patience amid the insults and sufferings inflicted on him. He replied simply and frankly, "My custom is to see myself, with regard to those who do such things, just like a puppy with regard to its masters." At these words I bowed my head and said to myself, "This brother has found the way." I made the

sign of the cross and left him, imploring God's protection on us both.

81. Sometimes the reason we do not get upset is our contempt for our brother, and this is clearly disastrous. But when we do get upset with a brother who ill-treats us, our perturbation may originate in momentary bad dispositions or in the dislike we feel for that brother. Very different reasons may also come into play. But if we carefully seek out the root cause of our disquiet, we always find the same: the fact that we do not practice self-accusation. This is why we feel crushed and never at peace. It is not surprising that all the saints say there is no other road than this. No one has found true peace by following any other road, and neither should we imagine we will find it if we never consent to accuse ourselves. Indeed, even were we to perform a thousand good works, if we do not follow the road of self-accusation we will not fail to suffer and to make others suffer, thus forfeiting all merit.

By contrast, what joy, what repose of spirit will be tasted, wherever he goes, by the man who accuses himself, as Abba Poemen says! He judges himself a priori to have deserved whatever injury, insult, or suffering he may meet and is never troubled or upset. What more carefree state could possibly exist?

82. But you may say: "If a brother is unpleasant to me, and on examining my conscience I find I have given him no cause, how can I accuse myself?" As a matter of fact, if anyone examines his conscience honestly and with the fear of God, he will certainly realize that he did give his brother cause, whether in word, action, or attitude. And if he really should find that in none of these ways did he give his brother cause in the present case, it is nevertheless very probable that he was uncharitable toward that brother on some other occasion, or that he made another brother suffer, and for that very fault, or for another sin he committed, he does deserve this present ill-treatment. Therefore, if we examine our behavior in a God-fearing way and scrutinize our consciences carefully, we will always find that we are responsible in some way.

It also happens that a brother, believing himself to be in a state of peace and tranquillity, is angered by an unfriendly word addressed to him by someone and considers that he is right to be angered, because he thinks: "If that person had not come and said that upsetting thing, I would not have sinned." That is an illusion and faulty reasoning. Did the person who said the word put the brother's passion into it? No, but by that word he simply revealed the passion that was already within the brother and of which the brother might repent if he wished. This brother is like a wheaten loaf that is beautiful on the outside, but when it is cut open is found to be moldy inside. He thought he was at peace, but there was a passion inside him that he did not know about or did not think important. A single word from his brother brought to light the moldiness in his heart. If he wishes to obtain mercy, let him repent, let him purify himself, and in the end he will see that he ought to be grateful to his brother for having been the cause of this improvement.

83. If we follow this path, trials will not be so overwhelming, and the further we advance, the lighter they will appear. Indeed, as our souls

grow, we become stronger and more capable of bearing everything that happens to us. Look at a beast of burden. If it is sturdy, it cheerfully carries the heavy burden that is loaded onto it; if it loses its balance it gets up straightaway and suffers no harm. If it is weak, however, any load is too much for it; and if it falls, it needs a lot of help to get back on its feet. The same is true of the soul. We are weakened every time we sin, because sin exhausts and corrupts the sinner. Anything at all is enough to overwhelm us then. But if instead we advance in virtue, what previously overcame us becomes more and more bearable. This is a great advantage to us, an abundant source of peace and progress, because it makes *us*, not other people, responsible for what happens, especially since nothing can happen to us without God's providence.

84. But someone might say, "How can I avoid being tormented if I need something and don't receive it? In that case, I am compelled by my need." But even then there is no reason for accusing someone else or being annoyed with someone. Someone who really believes he

needs something but does not get it should say: "Christ knows better than I whether I should obtain satisfaction, and he himself will take care of this thing or this food." The children of Israel ate manna in the desert for forty years, and even though it was of a single kind, for each of them that manna became whatever he desired: savory for the person who desired it to be savory, sweet for the person who desired it to be sweet, adapting itself to the temperament of each of them (cf. Wis 16:21). If, then, someone needs to eat eggs and receives only vegetables, let him say, "If it had been useful for me to eat an egg, God would certainly have sent me one. On the other hand, it is possible that these vegetables will be for me as though I were eating an egg." I am sure that this will be counted by our Lord as though it were martyrdom, because if a person is truly worthy to be heard, God will incline the hearts even of the pagans in order to show mercy to him according to his need. But if he is not worthy, or if what he prays for is not useful for him, he would find no satisfaction even if God made a new heaven and a new earth. It is true that sometimes we receive more than we need, and other times less. Since God in his mercy provides what is needful for each, if he gives more than enough, it is to show us the excess of his tenderness and to teach us to be grateful.

When, by contrast, God does not give even what we need, he supplements with his word the thing that is needed and teaches us patience. Thus, in all things, whether we receive good or evil, we should raise our eyes and thank God for everything that happens, never failing to accuse ourselves; and we should say with the Fathers, "If something good comes to us, it is by God's disposition; if evil comes to us, it is because of our sins."

Truly, all our sufferings come from our sins. The saints, when they suffer, suffer for the sake of God's name, or so that their virtue may be made manifest for the benefit of many, or for an increase of the reward that will come to them from God. But how could we say the same of ourselves, poor wretches that we are? Daily do we sin and let ourselves be ruled by our passions; we have left the straight path shown us by the Fathers that consists of accusing ourselves;

instead we follow the twisted path on which each accuses his neighbor. In all circumstances we are eager to blame our brother and impute faults to him. We live in carelessness, without concerning ourselves about anything, and yet we demand an account from our neighbor of how he is keeping the commandments.

85. Two quarrelling brothers came to see me one day. The older said of the younger: "When I give him an order, he gets annoyed, and so do I, because I think that if he had confidence in me and charity for me, he would willingly take in what I tell him." And the younger one said, "May Your Reverence forgive me: he certainly does not speak to me in a God-fearing way, but he wants to order me about, and that, I think, is why my heart has no confidence in him, according to the word of the Fathers."

We can see how these two brothers accused each other, and neither one accused himself.

Another two, who were each annoyed with the other, bowed reverently to each other but continued to feel angry. The first said, "He made me a reverence unwillingly, and that is why I have no confidence in him, according to the word of the Fathers." And the other said, "He was not charitably disposed toward me before I presented him with my excuses; therefore, I have no confidence in him either." Do you see the perversion of the human spirit? God knows how much it distresses me to see that we even use the words of the Fathers to serve our own bad will and ruin our souls.

What was needful was for each of them to accuse himself. One should have said, "I made the reverence to my brother against my will; therefore our Lord did not inspire him with confidence toward me." And the other should have said, "I was not charitably disposed toward him before the reverence he did me; and for that reason, God did not give him confidence in me." It would have been necessary for the first two to have done the same. One ought to have said: "I speak out of self-regard, and therefore God does not give my brother confidence in me." And the other ought to have said: "My brother gives me orders with humility and charity, but I am not docile or God-fearing." Whereas in fact, neither of them was on the right path; neither of them accused himself. On the contrary, each of them accused his neighbor.

86. This is the reason we do not manage to advance or become even moderately useful. Instead we spend our time in corrupting ourselves by thinking badly of one another and in tormenting ourselves. We each justify ourselves, we each neglect ourselves, as I have said, without noticing anything wrong; and instead, we prefer to demand an account from our neighbor of his observance of the commandments. And so we do not learn to do good; as soon as we receive a little light, immediately we call our neighbor to account and accuse him, saying: "He ought to do this; why did he do that?" But why do we not rather call ourselves to account over the commandments and accuse ourselves of not keeping them?

Let us recall the holy old man who was once asked, "Father, which part of this way do you consider to be the greatest?" He answered, "Self-accusation in everything." His questioner praised him, and the holy old man added, "There is no other way than that."

In the same way, Abba Poemen groaned and said, "All the virtues have entered into this house except one, and without that one, it is difficult for a man to stay upright." He was asked which virtue it was, and he replied, "Self-accusation."

Saint Antony said that man's main task was to take responsibility for his own wrongdoing in God's sight and to expect to be tempted until his last breath.

Everywhere, we find that the holy Fathers found peace of soul by observing this rule and referring everything, no matter how tiny, to God.

87. That was the reaction of a holy old man who was ill. His disciple put linseed oil, which is harmful, in his food instead of honey. The old man said nothing and uncomplainingly ate a first and then a second portion, as was necessary, without accusing his brother or attributing his action to malice and without saying a single word that might upset him. When the brother realized what he had done, he began to lament, saying, "I have given you death, Abba, and it was you who made me commit this sin by your silence."

But the old man said gently, "Do not lament, my son. If God had wanted me to eat honey, it would have been honey that you gave me." In this way he referred the whole matter to God.

But, good holy man, what did God have to do with all of this? Your brother committed an error, and you say, "If God had wanted …" What is the connection?

"Yes," said the old man, "if God had wanted me to eat honey, my brother would have given me honey."

He was sick and had been unable to eat for many days; and yet he was not angered at his brother, but, referring the matter to God, he remained calm. The old man spoke wisely, since he knew that if God had wanted him to eat honey, he would have changed even that foul oil into honey.

88. As for us, brethren, how often we turn against our neighbor and shower him with reproaches, accusing him of contempt and of acting against his conscience! Do we hear a word from our brother? Instantly we take it badly and say, "If

he had not wanted to wound me he would not have said that."

Think of the holy man who said, regarding Shimei, "If he is cursing because the Lord has said to him, 'Curse David,' who then shall say, 'Why have you done so?' " (2 Sam 16:10). Did God order a murderer to curse the prophet? How could God have said this to him? But in his wisdom the prophet knew well that nothing attracts God's mercy upon the soul as much as trials, especially those that come in time of misfortune and persecution. He also said, "Let him curse; for the Lord has bidden him." Why? "It may be that the Lord will look upon my affliction, and that the Lord will repay me with good for this cursing of me today." See how wisely the prophet acted. He was angered at those who wished to punish Shimei for cursing him: "What have I to do with you, you sons of Zeruiah?" he said. "Let him curse; for the Lord has bidden him" (2 Sam. 16:10–12).

How far we are from saying, with reference to our brother, "The Lord has told him to"! On the contrary, no sooner do we hear a word from our brother, than we react like a dog that has had a stone thrown at it: the dog leaves the person who threw the stone and goes and bites the stone. That is what we do: we abandon God, who allows trials to come upon us to purify us from our sins; and we fall on our brother, saying, "Why did you do that to me?" And when we could draw much benefit from those sufferings, we fall into traps of our own devising, by not recognizing that everything happens by God's providence, according to what is best for each person. May God give us understanding, through the prayers of the saints. Amen.

Other Excerpts from
Instructions and Letters
of Saint Dorotheus

9. [Speaking of Adam] When a man has no taste for self-accusation, he does not fear to accuse God himself.

[Speaking of Adam and Eve] But neither of the two stooped to accuse himself, and neither of them showed the slightest humility.

10. [Speaking of Adam and Eve] Now you see clearly the state we have arrived at, and to what innumerable evils we have been brought by our passion for justifying ourselves, denying our fault; confidence in oneself and clinging to one's own will are the offshoots of pride, the enemy of God. By contrast, the ways of humility are accusing oneself, distrusting one's own judgment, and hatred of self-will, and these things enable our nature to be restored and purified through Christ's holy commandments.

91. Abba Zozimus was once asked to explain the saying "Where there is no irritation, there is no combat." He said that if, at the beginning of a quarrel, when the smoke and sparks begin to appear, one takes the initiative by accusing oneself and abasing oneself before the flame of anger is lit, then one remains at peace.

101. Every sin originates in the love of pleasure, or in the love of money, or in vainglory. Lying, similarly, comes from one of these three passions. People lie either to avoid being accused and humiliated, or to satisfy a desire, or to achieve gain.

A liar's imagination is constantly at work, devising all possible subterfuges to attain his goal.

187. Fight to find a way of accusing yourself in everything, and hold fast to detachment toward knowledge.[8]

---

[8] "Detachment (*apsephiston*) toward knowledge" is not easy to translate, because it contains a wealth of analysis and experience (cf. I. Hausherr, *Penthos*). It could signify the total detachment that is manifested in the habit, or at least the resolve, not to want to give oneself, or to accept from others, praise for any kind of superiority (cf. I. Hausherr, *Direction spirituelle en Orient autrefois*).

Believe that everything that happens to us, even the tiniest details, comes from God's providence, and you will bear whatever comes to you without impatience. Believe that contempt and insults are remedies for your soul's pride, and pray for those who mistreat you, considering them true doctors. Persuade yourself that anyone who hates humiliation hates humility, and that everyone who avoids unpleasant people is avoiding sweetness.

Do not seek to know about the evil of your neighbor, and do not harbor suspicions against him. If your malice does give birth to suspicions, try to transform them into good thoughts.

196. Get it into your head that you have given pretext to temptation, even though at this moment you do not see why. Accuse yourself, have patience, and pray, and I am confident that our blessed Lord Christ will in his tenderness drive away the temptation.

30. In truth, nothing is more powerful than humility. Nothing is mightier than humility. If anything bad happens to the humble man, he immediately looks inside himself and judges

that he deserves it. And he does not permit himself to reproach anyone or throw the blame on another. He simply bears it, without upset, without annoyance, and in all meekness. Therefore "humility is not irritated and does not irritate anyone." The saint spoke truly: before anything else, we need humility.

63. Abba Poemen said that self-will is a steel wall between man and God. And he added, "It is a stumbling block", because it confronts God's will and sets up obstacles to it.

If a man renounces his own will, he can truly say, "By my God I can leap over a wall. This God—his way is perfect" (Ps 18:29–30). What admirable words! When one has renounced his own will, he travels the way of God without reproach. But if he obeys his own will, he cannot see that God's way is perfect. If he receives a rebuke or a challenge, he turns away in contempt and rebels. How could he listen to another or follow another's advice if he is clinging to his own will?

98. Never trust your suspicions, because a crooked measuring rod makes even what is

straight seem crooked. Suspicions are deceptive and harmful (this was a counsel from Abba John). Nothing is graver than suspicions. They are so harmful that in the long run they convince us and make us believe we have proof of certain things that do not exist and have never existed.

97. A man who admits suspicions is a liar in his thought. If he sees two brothers talking, he thinks, "They are talking about me", and if they stop talking, then he thinks it is because he is present. If anyone says a word, he suspects it is to offend him. In short, he suspects his neighbor in everything and says, "It is because of me that he did this; it is because of me that he said that." Such is the man who lies in his thought; he says nothing according to the truth, but all by conjecture. Here is the source of indiscreet curiosity, speaking badly of others, and the habit of going around eavesdropping, arguing, and judging.

Sometimes when a person fabricates suspicions, and the facts show that they are true, with the excuse of wanting to improve himself, the person goes around eavesdropping, telling himself, "When people speak against me, I will discover the fault that they see in me and can correct myself." But from the start, this attitude originates in the Evil One, since it is actually because of a lie that the person began to examine his conduct; in his ignorance he conjectured what he did not know. How can a bad tree produce good fruit? If that person really wants to correct himself, he will not be upset when some brother tells him, "Don't do that", or asks, "Why did you do that?" Rather, he will bow his head and thank him. Then he will improve. And if God sees that he desires to improve, he will not let such a person stray but will certainly send him someone to correct him. But as for saying "It is for the sake of my own amendment that I believe my suspicions" and going around spying on others, taking note everywhere—all of that is a false excuse inspired by the devil, who wants to deceive us.

100. Let us learn never to believe our suspicions. Nothing is more conducive to neglecting our own sins than that, because it leads us to

occupy ourselves constantly with what does not concern us. Nothing good comes of that, but rather a thousand problems, a thousand sufferings, and we never acquire the peace that comes of the true fear of God. Therefore when our interior untruthfulness sows suspicions in us, let us change them on the spot into good thoughts, and then they will not harm us. For suspicions and suppositions are full of malice and never leave our souls in peace. This is what is meant by being a liar in thought.

192. [A letter to a brother who asked him about insensitivity of soul and the cooling down of charity]

Against insensitivity of soul, my brother, it is useful to read holy Scripture continually, as well as the "catanyctic sayings" [sayings that elicit compunction] of the godly Fathers, which invite one to think of the terrible judgments of God and to remember that the soul will leave the body and meet the terrible Powers against which it has committed evil in this short and miserable life; that it will also appear before the terrifying and incorruptible tribunal of Christ to render an account before God, his angels, and every creature—an account not only of actions but also of words and thoughts. Remember constantly, too, these words that the terrible, just Judge will say to those on his left: "Depart from me, you cursed, into the eternal fire prepared for the devil and his angels" (Mt 25:41). It is also good to remember the great human tribulations, because in that way also the hard and insensible soul melts and becomes aware of its own unhappy state.

As for the weakening of fraternal charity, it comes from the fact that you consent to suspicious thoughts, and that you trust your own heart and wish to suffer nothing against your will. In the first place, you should, with God's help, pay no attention to your suspicions and rather apply yourself with all your strength to humbling yourself before your brethren and denying your own will for their sakes. If one of them insults or injures you, pray for him, as the Fathers have said, considering that such behavior will bring you great benefits and will cure you of the love of pleasure. If you follow that way, your anger will be calmed, since, according to the holy Fathers, charity "restrains anger". But above all pray to God to give you an alert and lucid spirit to discover the will of God and know what is good, what it is that God wants, what is the perfect thing to do (cf. Rom 12:2), and the strength to be ready and quick to undertake every good work.

Sayings

17. It is impossible to be angry against one's neighbor unless one has first arisen against him in one's heart and despised him, judging oneself superior to him.

18. If one is upset when one is corrected or accused concerning a passion, it is a sign that one possesses that passion voluntarily. By contrast, receiving the accusation or correction peacefully shows that one is free from that passion, or that if one has it, it is not voluntary.

20. Since we are victims of our passions, we should never absolutely trust what our heart tells us, because a crooked measure makes what is straight crooked.